2

<u>Further on Up the Road</u>

<u>(Rambling on!)</u>

By: Andrew D Siddle

© Andrew Siddle - All rights reserved on written poetry – 2nd July 2016

Contents

Friends on the Way.	Page 11
Spring Time Daffodils Arise.	Page 15
The Willows.	Page 19
Seagull.	Page 23
Come Up and See Me.	Page 27
West Ham Blues.	Page 31
I'll Light a Candle.	Page 35
Timble Down Tom.	Page 39
The Caudles.	Page 43
Aurora Borealis.	Page 47
Now Chill.	Page 51
Six a.m.	Page 55
Seeking the Wise Man of Leys.	Page 59
High Street Shuffle.	Page 65
Late Evening Blues.	Page 69
Bangers and Mash.	Page 73
Now Turn to Autumn.	Page 77
Another Day Gone.	Page 81
Lad's Night Out.	Page 85
On the Road to Somewhere.	Page 89
King of the Waves – Mannin Island.	Page 93
Acrostic Fontostique.	Page 97
Scrumpy Farm Blues.	Page 101
From the Heart.	Page 105
Angel of the Morning.	Page 109
Sweet Samantha.	Page 113
Christmas Carol.	Page 117
Dawn Chorus.	Page 121
Pendle.	Page 125
Searching for Me Pot of Gold.	Page 129
Tina.	Page 133
Toast to the Wild.	Page 137
North Sea Fish.	Page 141
Whitby.	Page 145
Under Cover of Night.	Page 149
Bogglin Billy - King of Norfolk.	Page 153
EE' Heck me Flies.	Page 157
Glastonbury Thorn.	Page 161
Hereward the Wake.	Page 165
The Songs I Once Knew.	Page 171
Esther.	Page 175
Across the Moors.	Page 179
Do you Believe?	Page 183
Rhiged of the Celts.	Page 187
Eye in the Sky.	Page 193
Caractacus of the Britons.	Page 197
Rainy Day Times - 3, 4, and 5.	Page 201
Cosmic Journey.	Page 205
The Oins of Nark.	Page 209
Just a Photograph.	Page 213
Time Tracked.	Page 217

Introduction

Introduction

Further on Up the Road is the third book of poetry that I have written since 1983. It's over three decades of writing poetry since I first started. I decided to do something special for the cover of the book this time. So I took a photograph of Rushton Road , between Desborough Town and Rushton village, in Northamptonshire. This is one of my favourite rural roads in Northamptonshire and passes by the Triangular Lodge , built between 1593 and 1597, which was designed and built by Sir Thomas Tresham. So here we have it! Poetry book three with lots of best of bits and pieces!

Friends on the Way

Friends on the Way

In my lifetime, so far, I have lived or worked in East London, Lancashire, Northamptonshire, Leicestershire, Birmingham City and Coventry City. I have also completed Foreign Office occasional armed Emissary work back in the mid 1980's. This was in the United States, Northern France, Spain, Italy and the UK. As you can imagine because of travel I have known a lot of people over time. Some just pass through a life and some stay friends a little longer. It is all part of the passage of time and part of life. Times change and move on and so do people. That is what this poem is about.

Friends on the Way

Of all the people I have known,
some have died and some have flown,
the best friends I once knew when small,
have gone on by to another call.
We mob of kids that roamed the streets,
annoying to some and buying sweets,
then the dizzy drunken days of pubs,
oh did they really call us thugs?
Acting a role for peers pro temp,
then life moves on and on again,
What is friendship really for?
To see us through our lifetime score?
Perhaps to help and share as one,
till our days are numbered; finally gone,
but the memories flow of golden hours,
funny tales; but time devours.
Maybe I'm just the gypsy kind,
roaming through all lives I find,
jotting down thoughts now and then,
of the souls I passed all through the glen.

Spring Time Daffodils Arise

Spring Time Daffodils Arise

Spring time again and what would spring be without the nodding heads of new born Daffodils shooting up from the soil . Every year without exception there they are; little yellow faces smiling up at everybody and worshipping the springtime sun.

Spring Time Daffodils Arise

How they come from deep in the ground,
green shoots unfurling to the dawning sun found,
uncurling a coil of sap driven green,
from deep below ne'er to be seen.

Now buds shake their heads to the rhythm of dawn,
good to be here and glad to be born,
and nodding their heads in agreement as one,
as the wind whistles by and surely is gone.

Slowly bursting to a yellow crown head,
all nod together in a golden flower bed,
all smiling on at those who pass by,
a golden array that catches the eye.

So praise the morning for this wondrous flower,
each day a dawning with a golden new power,
painting out green with a new golden brush,
yellow and clean and not there to rush.

The Willows

The Willows

One of my earliest memories is of walking by Willow trees bending down over the canal in the summer. There is something very magical about the Willow tree and it is truly different to other trees. To me a sight of the willow instantly generates a picture, in my head, of country walks going back to when I was only 7 years of age. I still remember willow branches bending down; and the leaves almost touching the canal water under the mid summer burning sun.

The Willows

Softly the willows bow their leaves,
to mirror a moment that no one perceives,
a gentle lament of a moment in time,
the breeze it sings for this moment I pine.
Beneath the willows a pool so deep,
images flash a mirror to keep,
your face in the water whilst ripples disrupt,
the willows bow low to the song they induct.
An eddying of time or a ripple of pool,
sent right back to a moment so cruel,
yet the years have passed as the ripples disperse,
so the face in the water mirrors a curse.
Now the wind and the wuthering sound again,
a distant whisper always the same,
reminding me now of all that was lost,
how could I know the true spirit's cost.
So the ripples of wind flow over hay,
and the low lying sun lights up the way,
the loss of a soul and the death of a heart,
but still the waves flow back to the start.

<u>Seagull</u>

<u>Seagull</u>

Memories of a holiday in Cornwall. I was there with a girlfriend whose family lived in Cornwall. All of a sudden a Seagull started to look menacing in close proximity to it's nest of eggs. I told my girlfriend to duck and get down into the sand but she refused saying "what are you on about?". 10 seconds later the Seagull landed on her head and plucked one of her eyeballs out. It then just flew off and left her lying on the sand crying with one eye missing. Poems about Seagulls therefore mean rather a lot to me.

This is a poem about a Seagull. But rather than just about a Seagull it is an inspiration from a band called Saturday Sun. They wrote a song called Seagull which I thought to be very haunting and very under rated. So here it is! A tribute to the band called Saturday Sun, from Swanage, called Seagull.

Seagull

A spring day and a Seagull flies,
eyes pierced by the grinning sun,
clouds so sparsely wind their way,
this canvass traversing as morning dies.

Gazing down at us all below,
freedom spreads it's wings and flows,
goes like an arrow free from it's bow,
striking the spirit in the life that we know.

Go Seagull and fly away,
fly high, fly sure, to another day,
go Seagull and fly strong,
fly on by those that stay.

Watching your wings now still as you glide,
the world below so small from your height,
soaring away to a far distant cliff,
your distant shelter and where you will hide.

Come Up and See Me

Come Up and See Me

When I wrote this I was remembering my time living on Teasal Way, in West Ham, East London. I remember that people, that I used to know from elsewhere, used to come over to London to visit me from time to time. Sometimes I liked chatting about old times. Other times I felt that I was being reminded of places and feelings that were not essential to my life anymore. (This is a photograph of Teasal Way).

Come Up and See Me

Come up and see me to talk of old times,
of folk we knew and the bell that chimes,
half a league on from where I have been,
half a league on from what you had seen.
To talk of moments trapped in space,
and idle gossip seen in it's place,
a time to wonder at all that's now past,
and all the faces I knew would not last.
People that came and people that left,
and all of those crimes that left us bereft,
what good is a memory if the whole lot were rot,
I'm better off out and keep what I've got.
So come up and see me and I'll feign a smile,
politely ignoring all of the while,
I once viewed the sun distant and high,
where it soars on to so shall I.

30

West Ham Blues

West Ham Blues

In the late 1980's my home was West Ham in the East End of London. It is difficult to capture the essence of modern day East London culture correctly in a poem. Modern day West Ham is nothing like the image presented in previous times. High speed bustle with on street hustle! I have tried to capture a bit of modern day East London in this poem anyway.

West Ham Blues

West Ham blues,
It's always in the news,
when it's all about surviving,
now you gotta choose.

Gi's your money mister,
so long to your sister,
walking by the pump house,
he aint even kissed her.

Spray paint on the wall,
but it took so long to call,
stroll; pump shoes and shades,
they're sure to make a' fall.

Dodgy dealing Ken,
it's really cheap at ten,
smoking roach tipped rollers,
then head back to the den.

Beer at the Swan,
then travel back for one,
all travel tube stacked,
the rail lines rumble on.

(Continued overleaf)

Wifi cheap at five,
but it's sure to be a dive,
fix your deals straight dude,
street wise for a skive.

West Ham news,
it's sure to give the blues,
when it's all about surviving,
now you gotta choose.

I'll light a candle

I'll light a candle

There is something magical about both candles and incense sticks ; preferably Sandlewood scented. Candlelit rooms seem to generate an alternative sense and feel. It is this alternative feel that generates a pleasant notion of fond memories. Also an image of good times somehow otherwise lost, in the back of the mind, during the mundaneness of everyday chores and tasks.

I'll light a candle

I'll light a candle as the daylight fails,

just watch the flicker and glow,

I'll see that candle burn to twilight,

just watch the starlight come around,

I'll watch that candle burn every hour,

just watch the moon rise full and round,

I'll see the candle melt right down,

just feel the depth of memories flow,

I'll see a flame die in darkest hour,

just sit here close then quietly go,

I'll see the cold wax molten around,

just leave my thoughts and inner glow.

Timble Down Tom

Timble Down Tom

Timble Down Tom? This is just a bit of non serious fun about a chap who lives in a shack. I've often thought how much good it would be to just move out to an old timber shack out in the back of beyond and get away from everything myself.

Timble Down Tom

Timbledown Tom,
lived in a Shack,
but didn't have the time to say.

The shack was tall,
whilst he was rather small,
the door racked rickets all the way.

With speeners on the roof,
they couldn't tell the truth,
the rackets wendled clearly all the day.

Windy wons asunder,
that never made a blunder,
all the young earchers chanced to stay.

Tin pot tied,
why old Timble almost died,
but saved by the cinders from decay.

Timbledown Tom,
lived in a shack,
but didn't have the time to say.

The Caudles

The Caudles

I spent many many hours walking when I was young. In the summer the best treat was to walk to to the top of the Langton Caudles which is part of the Leicestershire countryside from the days before I moved to Northants. The top of the Langton Caudles is marked by a Trig point and from this highest vantage point there is the clearest view, north, south, east and west possible to imagine. The word Langton means Long Town,(or Long house possibly in some cases) and all of the villages in the area take names such as Thorpe Langton, Church Langton, Tur Langton and others.

The Caudles

One leg against the farm gate and the other one on the ground. The sun was dazzlingly bright from the topside of the hilly field in front of me. I stood and wondered whether to cross or to continue walking further along the road a while. Three cars passed behind me; slowly along the country lane. Cows mooed nonchalantly in the field ; not really caring whether I entered their grassy homeland field or not.

I put my right foot up on the second highest bar of the gate and with my hands on top took a jump over. A jump over to follow the angled green footpath way marker to the top of my favourite hill.

The sun was sweltering and the flies were buzzing loudly. The sharp slope to the top left me breathless. I'd been on this route many times before but always, always, so stunning and scenic in summertime. From the top of the first hilly field the land then flattens out.Crossing a variety of arable and livestock fields, "wellie" mud sods and grass, the target is then in sight. Maybe three or so fields ahead a little iconic shadow on the horizon and there it is; the Trig point. Highest point of land and views that go on for forever and a day.

Reaching the height of the highest field I lay down on my back and melted into views that go on and on for forever. Lying and staring into the bluest depths above as cotton bud clouds drifted over.

Views north, south, east and west. Valleys
and farms, cloud shadows and sun, meandering
streams and distant rivers and flowing wind
whispering grass.

Surely; this is what summer is made for? If only the feel
of such a moment could carry on for lifetime; every day?
The feel of a little piece of Heaven on Earth for one
fleeting brief moment in time. Then gone again with a
blink as the day moves on by and sublime thoughts
descend once more to the mundane. Then the day moves
on and waiting chores call me back to home; back again.

<u>Aurora Borealis</u>

Aurora Borealis

Aurora Borealis. A mystic array of colours in a flashing neon lit sky. I once saw it from the County Cleveland coast in the distance. But this is nothing like the view from further north in Scotland. A wonderful thing to perceive; wonderful.

<u>Aurora Borealis</u>

Oh the Queen of Light she shot her bow,
and prisms abounded of light in the snow,
the darkened sky above so black,
burst into rays of colour like flack.
Her arrows filled the heavens high,
with blue and red and gold in the sky,
and shimmering light ; what a thing to perceive,
sparkling rays dance above trees.
The shimmering mystery of arrows above,
shot high over the nesting of doves,
and each arrow splinters to a cascading shower,
shining on with a sparkling power.
The colours reflect in the surf of high tide,
and the sea in the distance roars of it's pride,
the whole of the sky forms a magic array,
and here in our homes we stay well away.
The magic of fairies in a mystic light ray,
and the Queen of light rides in the fray,
a golden chariot with four horses drawn,
till all is gone and a new time is born.

50

Now Chill

Now Chill

I have always been a great believer in the value of meditation and stress minimisation skills. So much so that I even went to be taught breathing skills and self hypnosis at one time. Relaxation is so important in developing good, steady, decision making skills instead of being stressed out all of the while. This poem is about relaxation ....relax....relaaaaaax!

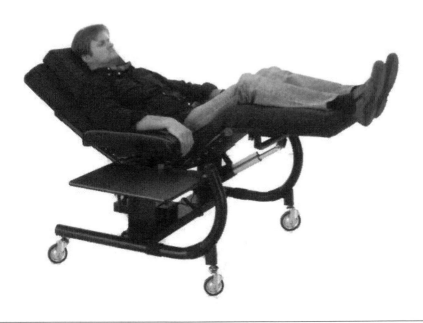

Now Chill

When the morning's work is well and done and
midday thoughts come through,

up turned toes and reclining views horizontally
stanced will do,

toes up high that reach for the sky slothing it back
with tea,

if all the world were so laid back then strife
would let us be,

slow your breath and forget the day just chill to
your heart beat bass,

let your spine go slack then lose the stress of all
your face,

if the world all snored we'd ne'r be bored so chill
and let it fall,

till back at last you'll work as fast fresh for works
old trawl,

(continued overleaf)

half an hour of chill for the power of rest at half
day break,

to renew the thrust of workday lust to a higher
level of stake.

Six a.m.

Six a.m.

It's amazing how people change. When I was a teenager 6 am in the morning was a nightmare time of day. It was a nightmare time of day because most people in my social group, at that time, didn't even venture a nose out of the bed clothes at that time of day. These days I positively love the early morning and always get about between 5 am and 6 am to start the first chores of the day.

Six a.m.

Early morning of the day,
the sunrise bright and here to stay,
darkened curtains tightly closed,
yawning out the yoodlies dozed.
Stretching arms and tired stares,
is breakfast on? It's time we shared,
razor blades and soggy towels,
garden birds that count the hours.
Six a.m. and all is well,
toast and jam we're doing swell,
coffee smells that fill the air,
with one sock on I couldn't care.
Where's my shirt I put it there?
It's fallen down behind the stairs,
is my tie tied up alright?
If they look at you they'll die of fright.
So off to work it's eight fifteen,
get the car it's nice and clean,
driving off to the highway long,
on to work in rush hour's throng.

Seeking the Wise Man of Leys (That's Beaumont Leys)

Seeking the Wise Man of Leys (That's Beaumont Leys)

Just before I wrote this I was sitting thinking of all the tales I had heard from the dark ages. In particular tales of visiting a wise sage or man of the woods for advice on what to do in life. Then I thought well; what if the wise man of the woods in the year 2016 actually lives in Beaumont Leys, Leicestershire. In a typical family minded , proud working culture, environment such as Beaumont Leys would there still be a queue of people coming to visit.? Or does it have to be a sacred special place , such as a woodland grove, before people take it seriously? Would the public , in their millions, trail to visit a 3 bedroomed Semi detached house next door to Beaumont Leys indoor Shopping centre? If not then why not?

The Wise Man of Leys (That's Beaumont Leys!)

I travelled near and I travelled far,
mostly guided by a star,
to seek that enigmatic bard,
that man who sees my every card.

I asked advice to find his lair,
and wondered at his fabled fayre,
that man of Leys with wisest face,
wise man of Leys I'd finally trace.

They told me "Leys?" what the 'eck,
it's Beaumont you want for yu' treck,
to Beaumont Leys I went to find,
the legend of this older kind.

At last my star shone strong above,
a sacred site most full of doves,
I ventured forth to find 'im there,
wise man of Leys with wisdom shared.

(continued overleaf)

"wise man of old I beg you please,
and this I do on bended knees,
tell me what me future be?
so I will know and I will see?"

The wise man with a gaze unbent,
stared at me in the time I spent,
then putting down his beer glass firm,
said this to me and made me squirm.

"Where's yu' from mate?" ; saideth he,
and belched a burp that was the key,
to all his wisdom deep inside,
in fright and awe I'd want to hide!

I said "from Flembeck on the Nazz",
"I live with me old wife called Mazz",
looking at me with a stare,
he said "I really couldn't care!"

Then pulling on his beer gut belt,
he shouted "get this nut now dealt!"
and cleared off back to whence he came,
there's nowt for him ; he's not the same".

(continued overleaf)

With these wise words I brightly went,
such wisdom in me time there spent,
the legendary wise man true,
with powers above both me and you.

High Street Shuffle

High Street Shuffle

This is a poem about frenetic city life. A busy high street, of an inner city district, that is so busy with things going on that there is no time to think. This could be New York City. This could be London. This could be Manchester. Where ever you feel it should be.

High Street Shuffle

Shuffle down the high street going to see Sam,
need a new jack file they're sure to see the plan,
new prams rolling and folk who are retired,
strolling down the pavement seeing who is wired.
Small kids, big wigs, mums out for a stroll,
office crowd gatherings and people on the dole,
chip fat, bean splats, ice cream lemon tops,
chinese takeaways you know it never stops.
Traffic lights on red the cars all in a line,
mobility chairs roll doing all just fine,
ciggies on the corner smoking by Al's store,
brown bag takeaways off licensed for some more.
Music bars howling the blues and rhythm timed,
listen to the chat lines who is it we'll find,
tall shops and offices paint and polished glass,
try old john's eatery it's going to be a blast.
Cleaners of the street brush and pick up trash,
while couples stand right by banking for more cash,
shoe leather pounding beat on concrete slabs,
see the new craze fashion you know it's all just fabs.

Late Evening Blues

Late Evening Blues

Wandering about pondering over things is something that I have always been guilty of. Often to the annoyance of others. This is a limerick....I think I've done three limericks in with my poems here and there!

Invented by the Irish at Limerick as a type of competition style of poetry the Limerick follows strict rules:-

* It must always be 5 lines long.
* Lines 1, 2 and 5 must rhyme with one another.
* Lines 3 and 4 must rhyme with each other.
* It must have a distinctive rhythm.
* It must normally be funny.

Late Evening Blues

I was walking in Stratford quite late,
wondering at London's old fate,
my girl she stormed out,
and started to shout,
get back inside it's too late.

Bangers n' Mash

Bangers n' Mash

Where would British people be without bangers n' mash? Second only to the quintessential fish n' chips. Could life really be possible without a greasy Lincolnshire or Cumberland and maybe a side portion of baked beans, or onion gravy, if you prefer?

Bangers n' Mash

They said it's a smash,
the rest are just trash,
so give me a bash,
a bash at the mash,
bangers n' mash,
the smash for a thrash,
it's bangers n' mash for me.

Bangers galore or you'll be a bore,
eat them alone or maybe for four,
gravy or mustard and onions fried,
a man with no bangers is one who died,
give it a smash for bangers and mash,
sing to the moon for this greatest tune,
it's bangers n' mash for me.

The smell of sausage fills the skies,
don't say there's none or you I'll despise,
the greatest sausage a Cumberland feast,
or how about Lincoln large as a beast,
swirl that gravy and let off some steam,
bangers that sizzle it's just like a dream,
it's bangers n' mash for me.

(Continued Overleaf)

Sizzling and spitting they leave the pan,
lashings of gravy until I'm a fan,
brown and chunky under my knife,
that's five for me and two for the wife,
dollops of mash that lump on my plate,
bangers and mash is truly my fate,
it's bangers n' mash for me.

Now Turn To Autumn

Now Turn To Autumn

Autumn gold and reds. The sublime majesty of leaves falling, and gradual decay, as nature gets ready for her next winter time snooze. The crisp leaves to trample under foot and the low lying shadowed sun. Riches beyond measure!

Now Turn To Autumn

Whilst autumn leaves they start to turn,
the browns and reds of seasons beauty,
with moss around we start to yearn,
of the death of summer in Autumn's duty.

Slowing down to a golden sun,
the time turned seasoned nature's rule,
shadows grow as day is done,
and dew drops glisten in mornings cool.

The melancholy law of summer's decay,
frost is set for breakfast sights,
while shadows long draw us to stay,
warm inside whilst strong winds blight.

My soul flies with autumn bird calls,
soon to be gone to distant lands,
as leaves now rustle and finally fall,
maybe some day I'll join their bands.

Another Day Gone By

Another Day Gone By

Remember how days seemed to last forever at Primary School? To me the three months summer holiday from school seemed to last a year. Then one day I started work; and all of a sudden not only did time start to flash by but every year seemed to be what had previously felt like three months.

(Illustration from the classic film – the Time Machine)

Another Day Gone By

Slowing down at the end of the day,
the old clock chimes in a chilled out way,
as my mind slows down with the chores now done,
laid back thoughts by the sinking sun.
Winding down as the streets go dark,
silhouetted trees now strikingly stark,
heading home hearts of the evening shift,
while my thoughts meander and start to drift.
Feet up on the bed while listening to time,
it passes slowly with no reason or rhyme,
plans for tomorrow what will they bring,
when the world awakens and the blackbirds sing.
So for now I'll lie and deeply think,
slowing my breathing and sip a drink,
music in the distance of this evening's beat,
dozing asleep whilst staring at my feet.

Lad's Night Out

Lad's Night Out

From my teens to my early twenties the twice weekly lad's night out was a quintessential part of my life. I particularly liked my regular pub the Talbot. The Talbot was home to a motor bike club and even I had a grey coloured bike by the age of 17/18; grey being the colour of the paint work to the petrol tank with a shiny silver make plate over this. How on earth I ever managed to get up the following morning, with the amount I used to drink, is beyond rhyme or reason. Obviously we walked to the pub when drinking! We used to do Whisky Chasers. So it was one single neat whisky to put down with each, and every, pint of bitter ale purchased.

Lad's Night Out

Give me a pint with a frothy head,
with rare old hops for the taste buds fed,
and give me a brew that came from the cask,
a full bodied ale for which I can ask,
Malted barley always the tops,
taking a gulp that never stops,
beery, bleary, pints galore,
bitter ale a best pint score.
London Pride or Furkin Best,
Pedigree or John Smith's zest,
smell the hops all malty free,
a pint for you and two for me.
So line 'em up a bar time treat,
clinking glasses and shuffling feet,
all for us till final bell,
then scuffle home the nights been swell.

On the Road to Somewhere

<u>On the Road to Somewhere</u>

I wrote this when I was sitting thinking about the old song by Talking Head called On the Road to Nowhere. As somebody who travels around I'm into roads; and I'm into the idea that every journey in life should lead to somewhere. I don't believe in journeys without reason. I don't believe in travelling on roads that have no final destination.

On the Road to Somewhere

On the road to somewhere distant ahead,
a far distant vista both new and unsaid,
onward and forward or be left behind,
time is a calling for all that we'll find.

Just a little further it's over the hill,
I'll ride on much faster just for the thrill,
bouncing through pot holes a rough ride road,
but the future is calling in all we've been told.

I'll lower my visa against the sun's gleam,
riding much faster to a lifestyle unseen,
leaving the past for others to hold,
our dead are gone not here to behold.

So I'll sing you a song of Oasis in time,
a place to move on to for the past's just a bind,
joyful in finding that yesterday's gone,
all of those bad times resigned to a song.

So give me the morning and an open road,
my future is dawning not here to be sold,
A cloud of dust is all you will see,
then that is me gone for the new place to be

King of the Waves
(Mannin Island)

King of the Waves (Mannin Island)

The Isle of Man is said to have been named after one of it's first early leaders called Manannan Mac Lir. Manannan was one of the early military leaders of the Tuatha De Danann tribes of the west; whose people moved west after the loss of North African territories including Carthage. Also of course the sea faring fleet of Tarshish in southern Spain, Sidon and Tyre in Phoenicia, and many others in the Mediterranean lands. This is a poem about Manannan.

King of the Waves (Mannin Island)

A long way from Mannin in the island of old,
rides Manannan Mac Lir a spirit so bold,
on the three waves of Erin when storms do arise,
whilst the spirit of Fand his wife sobs and cries.
Buried at Tonn Banks so near Donegal,
but his dead steed Enbarr gave up the call,
it's master now gone and Manx a lost race,
so the surf frothed waves gather in pace.
King of all Manx where he once reigned,
now lost in time to the changes since feigned,
captured by Ireland his spirit now seen,
he rides the storm waves in these places been.
His cloak of Mists thrown to the tide,
in this place of rest where he finally died,
his breast plate blown with rust by the sea,
his spear now broken; no longer to be.
Now as the lightning strikes out at rocks,
and waves now plunder with thunderous plots,
at the height of this roar of thunder and waves,
his wife screams loudly the name in the caves.
Hidden forever by Donegal's coast,
the body of Manannan releases it's ghost,
seen by the sailors and watchmen of night,
and seagulls fly over screaming in fright.

(Continued from previous page)

Notes

Manannan's full title was Lord of the Sea as was very common for many early heroes with connections to Carthage, Phoenicia, the sea princes and indeed the earlier Hittite tribes of the Mediterranean coastland hinterlands before Phoenicia.He knew his wife Fand as Pearl of beauty which was his name of affection for her.

Manannan had three sons called Ilbhreac, Fiachna and Gaidiar. Also a foster son called Lugh. He also had three daughters called Aine, Aoife and Griane.

Manannan was a powerful early sea faring leader and one of the first strong kings of the Isle of Man or Mannin Island home of the Manx Celt tribes.His royal fortress was on the top of Barrule. He also held court at Cronk Y Voddy.

He was killed in battle fighting the Irish tribes, for Manx Island, at the battle of Magh Vuillen and was buried by Uillenn Faebarderg at Tonn Banks near to the coast of Donegal.

Acrostic Fontostique

Acrostic Fontostique

Where would we be with out the good old acrostic for a bit of poetic fun? Here is another one called Buy Me a Burger. I can't quite remember why I wrote it so it must be that I was feeling hungry at the time.

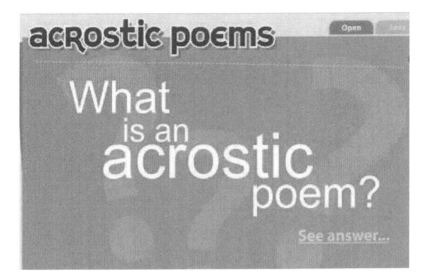

Acrostic Fontostique

B   eing hungry is no crime in itself
U   nless one has already eaten of course.
Y   ears of improvement to fast food cuisine

M   ean that any town high street hosts
E   xcellent choice and tasty variety;

A   nd there are almost certainly

B   ountiful quantities of world class cuisine
U   nless one is short of cash in which case
R   eturn home and hit the freezer big time.
G   enerous portions of frozen chips and burgers lie
E   choing desires of gluttonous scoffing and
R   evelry hidden below the excitement of a
     freezer top lid.

Scrumpy Farm Blues

Scrumpy Farm Blues

I remember teenage days on holiday in Cornwall with friends. Every day seemed to involve visits to the local scrumpy apple cider farm before heading down to the sandy beach with a bag full of tiddie oggies. Believe me with the strength of scrumpy that we used to buy; lying down on the beach was the best possible decision after swigging from a scrumpy flagon.

Scrumpy Farm Blues

Swirling my flagon while crossing the gate,
the smell of sweet apples cemented my fate,
leaving the farm shop so distant behind,
this scrumpy farm sale just made up my mind.

I stopped by a stile to take a swig,
then belched out loudly just like a pig,
that sweet trickly apple juiced down my throat,
and I stared at a hay stack next to a goat.

One swig more and my eyes spun round,
just one swig further my feet left the ground,
was that a cow speaking to me?
Why did that goat just ask me to tea?

Standing up, no! Perhaps I'll sit down,
Scrumpy green clouds swirling around,
well just one more sip and then I'll go home,
then standing up straight I fell on a gnome.

Three steps on then I fell in a trough,
a horse stood laughing and started to scoff,
but the clouds in my eyes were swirling so fast,
now where is me flagon I'll drink till the last.

So here is the lesson for true scrumpy time,
don't try to stand just lie in a line,
for when old Scrumpy hits the right spot,
you'll be lucky to stand so stay in your slot.

Lying down flat is the best way to drink,
old scrumpy man's fallen oh wouldn't you think,
apples and papples and fwizzy man times,
just swig your flagon and hear the bell chimes.

From the Heart

From the Heart

On the subject of dating, and going on dates, I had an interesting time when I first started. My life was one of travel, changing locations and roles in life, and always struggle. Perhaps more so than most. This is just maybe a small poem about that.

From the Heart

I gave it all from the heart,

and what did I get back,

A smite in the face or a proverbial wack.

Sometimes working; & sometimes sleeping rough,

what does it mean when the world is saying tough!

Wandering down a lane or dreaming of the hills,

but you just accused me of seeking cheap thrills.

From the heart is where it came,

and I now want it back,

rolling down the lane and racing down the track.

Lace my boots to the road and polish off the dust,

consign you to a thought and let the moment rust.

Angel of the Morning

Angel of the Morning

This is a play on the words/feelings of a song called Angel of the Morning. The version of this song by Chrissie Hynde , and the Pretenders, has always been a favourite of mine. I guess this is a tribute to the song. The song holds special personal feelings for me in it's words. There was once an amazing live version played on the American TV series Cheers.

Angel of the Morning

Angel of this darkened hour,
take your freedom from this power.

Bound as one or free to run,
love ties on when all is done,
two hearts as one or outward bound,
to be so true or never found.

Angel of this darkened hour,
take your freedom from this power.

A stroke of cheek or kiss so true,
you to her or she to you,
sinners of the dawn to break,
love found all and not a fake.

Angel of this darkened hour,
take your freedom from this power.

The sun it shines in darkened shade,
dim dawn's new and misty haze,
she wanted all but asked for none,
stay or go you are the one.

Angel of this darkened hour,
take your freedom from this power.

The years go by and on and on,
the scars of time show all and one,
you turn from her and walk away,
but never will she plead you stay.

Angel of this darkened hour,
take your freedom from this power.

Sweet Samantha

Sweet Samantha

Spring to summer ever year and sway hipster jean clad girls roam town centre and city streets; but the song is always the same. The desire to be centre of attention, and when all is said and done, dancing queen in the nightclub or disco. The one dream of all young females. To be the centre of attention and best on the dance floor.

Sweet Samantha

Samantha's away, hipping down the road, with looks that make many men fight.

With denim tight sways, that always cause delays, hip sway time from left to right.

Belly button showing, over muffin top a' flowing, passing by all just like a star,

Then hip struck slink, for complete and utter kink, has our Sam really gone too far?

Stilettos click, and dance lights flick, and the lads all really want some more.

Showing all her curves, for those "who has the nerves", Sam's there dancing at the core.

She spins way round, hipping all the time, showing how much more there is in store.

Sweet Sam sways, but never really stays, when the music stops she's always out 'the door,

Flirting for the joy, that she well knows, if you don't dance you're really just a bore.

Christmas Carol

Christmas Carol

Christmas time for carols and rhyme. Maybe a little of the favourite beverage too many? What if Father Christmas did that instead of delivering your long awaited prezzie? Old Santa on the mulled red wine but don't tell me I'm doin' fine!

Christmas Carol

Christmas cards and mulled red wine,
mince pies stacked we're doing fine,
fairy lights that dance and blaze,
Mistletoe to kiss and praise.
But Santa stumbled on the roof,
with too much beer they needed proof,
sliding in a drunken daze,
he hit the concrete in a haze.
The police they nicked him on the lawn,
swearing blind his red hat torn,
falling o'er the neighbours cat,
it wouldn't have been if he weren't fat.
Swearing at the sergeant too,
he took a swing and hit a few,
so now he's locked up in the 'nick',
no 'prezzies' for us he's got the kick!
Now we sit and watch the snow,
Santa's gone as well we know,
locked up with the drunk tank sick,
they fired the chap for being thick.
As evening dusk brings Christmas lights,
our son Johnny dies in fright,
"where's Santa gone it's Christmas time!"
"Naw....'ee's 'gone down' 'ee's doin' time!"
So Santa's charged with 'G.B.H.',
no time now; for Rudolph's mates,
the judgment said it truly is,
Santa's 'banged up' on the fizz!

Dawn Chorus

Dawn Chorus

Dawn; a magical time of day with the sun rising, the birds starting to call, and sleep gradually rolling back to consciousness like a tidal wave over a sand bank. This is a poem about the dawn time awakening of a new day.

Dawn Chorus

Lay the sheets all around,
and hold me close,
till all is found.

The night that takes all,
from our mortal caress,
till daylight arrives,
and finds us undressed,

The birds that awaken,
in the early hours of dawn,
had not foreseen,
all we had known.

Lay the sheets all around,
and hold me close,
till all is found.

Pendle

Pendle

This is a poem about the trial and hangings of the Pendle witches , in Lancashire, in the year 1612. I was born in Lancashire , in the town of Padiham, so the Pendle witches story holds a special fascination to me. In fact I used to be taken up to Pendle Hill, now and then, when I was a child because we only lived a few miles away.The witch trials commenced after a long standing famous feud between two families. On one side the Demdike family and on the other side the Chattox family.

Pendle

Stark on the horizon but yellowed with sun,
the mound of old Pendle saw what was done,
and old Pendle sits surrounded by fields,
an old man's hunch back cursed in deaths yields.

The witches who hung silhouetted in spite,
swung in their death robes from left to right,
but the wind whistles sweetly of all these times past,
with the passing of time she's there till the last.

The family of Demdike and Chattox fought sore,
a feud full of fighting brought death to the door,
cursing each other and poisoning clear,
with death and black magic that brought so much fear.

Clay figures and pins and illness so caused,
the Reaper set free and so never paused,
now the clouds pass over Pendle's height,
and wander the sheep bleating with might,

They remember not Chattox; witch of the night,
nor the family of Demdike; of whom she did fight,
twelve were accused with terrible tales,
of witches and magic and spells that n'er failed.

Nine women, two men, found guilty when done,
and ten of them hung right under the sun,
so the shadows grow from the Pendle mound,
and the wind whispers on of all it had found.

As the evening clouds cast a darkness below.
the darkness is found from the dusk to bestow,
an eeriest feel of a fracture in time,
and a flicker of shadows hanging in prime.

Searching for me Pot of Gold!

Searching for me Pot of Gold!

Who wouldn't want that gorgeous pot of gold sitting at the end of the rainbow beyond the bottom field. Red and gold and all colours there; plenty of coins of gold to share. Get your spade out and get out there and find it!

Searching for me Pot of Gold!

I have heard long ago at whatever the cost,
to find the true power of the rainbow lost,
and in the dark morn of spring for to see,
the ice crystal prisms of colour to be.
For the old all new the secret so free,
the gold for to find where the colours shall be,
so I takes me gold in a pot so tall,
and searches for the place to buries it all.
For I knew completely that I would see,
at the end of the rainbow there should it be,
so what better place to bury me treasure,
investing in future for good times of leisure.
So the new rain of morn makes light crystals dance,
and I see a rainbow that points with a glance,
to me pot of gold out there in the ground,
hidden in grasses most ne'r to be found.
Looking out through a crack in the glass,
my window crumbles time sent to smash,
but there in the distance I truly see, me pot of gold;
pointed at for free.

Tina

Tina

The best memories in life are often of the first person in life to really make a difference to us. The memory of that first special person can be something to treasure. However; when time proves to show that people surrounding that special person had no other desire in life than to be control freaks something else is demonstrated. What is demonstrated is that freedom of thought of the individual is the most precious gift to mankind! Anybody who tries to take away that precious gift should be belittled and put down. Freedom of thought, of the individual, is a special gift given by God and it is not for other people to try to take it away.

Tina

There once was a girl who held my hand,
the reason why I couldn't understand,
but somewhere in her heart she found,
some side of me that seemed to astound.

I couldn't see what is was back then,
and as time went by we met again,
older now and more mature,
but once again a love so pure.

From 8 years old until the last,
a purest soul with love in her eyes,
so when they took her I felt it too,
for all she felt I felt true.

No chance in life and hurt so bad,
she promised to give all she had,
but I wanted nothing but to see her eyes,
then they took those as well so now I despise.

We were young then but quickly old,
secret thoughts remained untold,
but to me one day when I look to the skies,
I'll see her again and those deepest eyes.

Toast to the Wild

Toast to the Wild

I was brought up with a healthy appetite for nature and anything that is naturally wild. Also a view that anything wild is part of a cosmic consciousness. A cosmic conciousness that controls vegetation, flowers, wild animals and evolution. So if I ever seem wild myself this is because I am tuned in, in thought, to the rustle of leaves and scurrying of field mice. What could be more natural?

Toast to the Wild

Wildness in my heart,
wildness in my soul,
wild bred ways in sight,
wild bred ways in store.

The heather blew as rabbits fled,
the sky above turned grey and bled,
bled for all the wild born free,
a different notion some might see.

I followed the river seeking the wild,
but emptiness was all I found,
though somewhere in the distant fields,
I thought I'd found it quite concealed!

As the snow topped mountain peered down,
a soaring Eagle wore the crown,
of all the wilderness below,
this bird soared by with regal glow.

Of mice and men and bitter fights,
of wilderness and darkened nights,
of nature's spirit deep inside,
and all the thoughts we try to hide.

(Continued overleaf)

Let my soul fly high and proud,
way above the babbling crowd,
for every wild blown thought of man,
was surely part of nature's plan.

So find a road and a will to go,
to wander off with wildest flow,
the joy of finding new found sights,
and the joy of travel and open nights.

To explain a thought of wild flung man,
following nature's every plan,
but deep inside is surely seen,
God's own mirror in all that's been.

Wildness in my heart,
wildness in my soul,
wild bred ways in sight,
wild bred ways in store.

North Sea Fish

North Sea Fish

Whilst I was born in Lancashire, North West England, a major part of my family were born in the north east. There used to be a really major fishing culture along the coast of the north east in previous centuries. There are many tales of children dancing in the streets upon the coming home of the local fishermen, with their catch, back to north east shores. That is what this poem is about.

North Sea Fish

Dance in the street till the grey nets bring back the haul,
fishmongers treat till the deals are done one and all,
Aran sweaters and wool hats fill the sea scored shore,
Breakers beat and surf swirls round once more.

The deepest blue of northern seas of deep.
then bobbing boats trawl the fish nets steep,
grey skies scream and seagulls seek to keep,
all that is left of the treats seen there to eat.

The silvery moon shadows yesterdays dreams of all,
salt and ozone mix the Herring smell of trawls,
then away once more ; another day gone by,
fish shops sent today's new catch to fry.

144

<u>Whitby</u>

<u>Whitby</u>

Although not recently I have visited Whitby Harbour, in north east England, many many times. The fishing community culture is stronger here, arguably, than anywhere else in England. The smell of ozone, salt, freshly caught sea fish, sizzling frying fish and chips combine with the smell of ozone, sea salt, and sea breezes. The experience is one not to be missed.Whitby has an historical reputation, and history, of smuggling. This prose poem is a little bit about that.

Whitby

It's 1773 and the North Sea fog is as thick as smoke; but the fog rolls over the brashness of sea spray ravaging the moorings as creaking boats rock back and forwards. Mooring ropes croak and strain in the semi darkness but a light strikes the harbour from the Abbey high above.

Way ahead in the Fog, out in the turbulent blackness, the silhouette of a monster. A monster blocking out the dusk horizon ahead of this seascape with it's square set sails billowing out over a 150 ton hulk. 18 six pounders point arrogantly towards the shore awaiting any sight or sound from Government Revenue Cutters. Orders already given to the 25 strong Kent men crew as to what to do on sighting.

So now here come the cobbles. A myriad of tiny small sploshing vessels head noisily splashing towards a swinging lantern in the distance. Brandy, whisky, and tea crated and waiting in the darkness beyond the swinging light. An army of cobble oars and rowers armed with bludgeons; all heading towards their night time planned goal.

Now the gulls noisily awake soaring above to a much higher height; all woken by the noisy din of oars heading out from smugglers bliss. Suddenly a cannon sounds in the distant dark. A lantern swings it's final triumph and cobbles scurry back to the shore line. Scurrying like red ants back to the comfort of the nest. Yet two hours still wait till day break!

Under Cover of the Night

Under Cover of the Night

In the 1980's I undertook occasional Foreign Office armed civil service/Emissary projects having completed full training in firearms over a period of time. My Emissary work amounted to various projects with expenses paid for by Foreign Office, Section Six, and the British Embassy. The projects ended up being mostly in summer months and I undertook armed Emissary work in Italy, Spain, Northern France, the UK for a couple of projects or so, and the USA. My training was the culmination of my time with RAF Cadets 1084 Squadron as a youngster combined with further training with the Army Arms Training Centre, the M.O.D., Civil Service Arms Training Centre, and an Italian Police Arms Training Range for my project in Italy. It was during my time in the USA that I developed sun stroke whilst riding a two and a half day trip across the whole of the United States on motorbike to my eventual destination New York City. The sun stroke led me to hearing the desert sands whispering whilst trying to sleep in the desert overnight. America was also where I was filmed by a United States private film/News company who interviewed me on the road whilst I was riding my motorbike toward New York City.

Under Cover of the Night

I spun my motorbike around from the highway
accelerating until the group of people seeking
me became a murmur of voices behind me.
Over a sand bank then winding my bike wheels
through sand and cactus and scrub; and oh the
joy of the freedom as the bike wheels bounced
the sand and I felt the biggest of smiles grow on
my face. I got what I wanted and I got what I
needed; the feeling of real freedom. The voices
of the small group of people seeking me in the
distance seemed to get louder again so I looked
to the horizon and saw a cliff face all red and
gold under the afternoon sun. I revved my
engine and headed for the cliff one mile away
straight over the desert sands. Oh what a joy
was that bouncy one mile over the sands and
scrub. The sun heavily tanning my already sun
burnt face.

I had no water, no food, no sleeping bag and no
means of lighting a fire and I was as happy as a
sand pixie. Night time drew and nobody else
came to try to find me.Hidden beyond the cliff
escarpment I happily watched the stars traverse
the Heavens and was lamented by irritable
crickets scratching noisily until they too became
drowsy.

(Continued overleaf)

At four in the morning I opened my eyes ; my motorbike
still next to me. The sands had turned to
dead as all insects had burrowed their way to deep
sleep. The sky was now totally blackened; I
supposed because of clouds stealing the very jewel
of night from the stars. All of a sudden the sands
seemed to start to whisper with a murmur.

In the absence of insect scratchings and calls there
seemed to be whisperings and mutterings coming
from below the sands. Every time I heard a whisper
I turned on my motorbike headlights. Every time
the whispering stopped I turned the the lights off
again. All of a sudden I felt such fear that I put my
bike lights on fully for a whole two hours.

Two hours later I bounced my way back over the
sands to the highway aiming for the distant New
York City; but still I wanted to go back and see and
hear! Would the sands still whisper to me or was it
just me? Sun stroke or primordial hauntings from a
distant time ? One day I'll go back to those sands
and then I'll know.....one day.....one day I'll
know............

Bogglin' Billy – King of Norfolk

Bogglin' Billy – King of Norfolk

There are Kings and there again are Kings! Some Kings are appointed as royalty and some are locally selected as folklore heroes. Bogglin Billy is a local Fen folklore hero. This poem is about Bogglin Billy; The King of Norfolk.

Bogglin' Billy – King of Norfolk

Reed man Ray had not that much to say as I meandered my way down through the Broads.

But Bogglin Billy was the son of old man Dilly and Ray new all the flat land fords.

The reed land Fen had a very strong leader & Bogglin' Billy was he named.

King of Norfolk as birds fly crowfoot for Billy reigned proud against the shamed.

He was treated with respect though he never was well kept and leader of the Fen was he.

When belching in the bar our Billy was the star and fed on pickled eggs to stay.

Many people wonder why Bogglin' got his title but it's kept a fenland secret to this day.

Though I'll tell you the tale if you keep it all within and tell no other soul that way.

Long ago there was arson and the local store was raided by a group of young thugs to stay.

(Continued overleaf)

Bogglin' was there with a very dark stare and in the queue for pickled eggs that day.

Now belchin' Billy was known for flatulence and few believe what they saw as true.

For a petrol bomb it landed and all five lads were stranded as Bill's gas blew they flew.

With the five lads dead why old Bill became the head and King of Fen till final tide.

The sea comes and goes lashing on the coast but Bill's pickles are famous for all time.

King Bogglin' Billy the hero of the Fen & King of all the reedland thinks!

Hero till final tide when the earth it finally sinks and Bogglin' sits pickled in his stinks.

EE' Heck Me Flies

EE' Heck Me Flies

This is another little bit is silliness set in Harrogate. Harrogate is a town in North Yorkshire. Not to be taken too seriously as many will now; I'm not into seriousness, all of the while , and seriousness isn't what these little books of poetry are for.

EE' Heck Me Flies

Walking through the mall for shopping one day,
well it seemed quite nippy with a breeze all the
way,I wandered around just looking for a kipper,
when I heard a shout from a rather small nipper:

EE' heck your flies
I said "you what?"
EE' heck your flies
well what had I got?

Looking down low I saw my zip was down,
so slank by the burgers with a very big frown,
my zip was caught by my pants beneath,
me best "Y" fronts and beyond belief.

I turned round just tugging at my zip,
and grunted at the sound of an awesome rip,
just then a girl from checkout number three,
walked around the aisle and headed straight for
me.

EE' heck your flies,
I said "you what?"
EE' heck your flies,
Well what had I got?

(Continued overleaf)

Hearing a shriek from the girl of checkout three,
security were called and had me on me knee,
just as I thought my time was done,
security just grunted "you doing this for fun?"

EE' heck me flies,
He said "you what?"
EE' heck me flies,
well what have you got?

So hiding my trouble behind a bag of frozen
chips, I was scanned out by checkout & almost
swayed me hips, dashing for my car and
panting all the way, but the traffic warden saw
and promptly came to say.

EE' heck your flies,
I said "you what?"
EE' heck your flies,
well what had I got?

So driving back home with a caught broken zip,
with me pants caught firmly for a really long
trip, well why does it happen when I'm trying to
be good, with my pants in my zipper ; not the
way that they should.

Glastonbury Thorn

Glastonbury Thorn

Some people hold Glastonbury in high esteem and for good reason. The heart of English Celtic Culture has a special place inside for this location. Joseph of Arimathea planted his walking staff here, a long time ago, and miraculously it started to grow again and became a new thorn bush in time. Also modern English citizens seem to have decided that Glastonbury Tor is the site of what was called Avalon Island. If one studies the history books, and actual evidence, then it is almost certain that Avalon Island is actually the old Knights Templar island called Lundy. Not that it matters; Glastonbury Tor is easier to get to as a lucrative tourist destination site for holiday makers.

Glastonbury Thorn

A long while ago in the ancient mists,
came a man from afar to the hill of views,
in Glastonbury's fields he thrust his fists,
down with a staff of true born news.

There from this staff the green leaves sprouted,
and in this growth turned a trunk of new,
the people around swore they never doubted,
a miraculous thing and it flowered true.

Flowering in winter and again in spring,
a wondrous Hawthorn of distant shores,
Joseph's gift to be fit for a king,
Arimathea's visit for the long lost cause.

Once a year it's blossom is sent,
to the Monarch of present on the throne,
a true born blessing of old times spent,
a gift from the wild not to be owned.

Of all the centuries rolling on by,
a simple Hawthorn passed the test,
a symbol to people of unity high,
a single bush mirroring quest.

Notes

The Thorn Bush once attacked and cut down by Oliver Cromwell as a symbol of superstition in his mind... Also cut down by vandals...Also cut down by anti British culture supporters....yet still we have more cuttings of the original bush of Joseph on their way; and one also remains in Washington DC, USA.

The Glastonbury Thorn is a form of Common Hawthorn, Crataegus monogyna 'Biflora'1 (sometimes incorrectly called Crataegus oxyacantha var. praecox), found in and around Glastonbury, Somerset, England. Unlike ordinary hawthorn trees, it flowers twice a year (hence the name "biflora"), the first time in winter and the second time in spring. The trees in the Glastonbury area have been propagated by grafting since ancient times.1 This type of Hawthorn is unusual because it flowers twice per year where as others do not. IT flowers once in winter and then again in spring time.

It is associated with legends about Joseph of Arimathea and the arrival of Christianity in Britain, and has appeared in written texts since the medieval period. A flowering sprig is sent to the British Monarch every Christmas. The original tree has been propagated several times, with one tree growing at Glastonbury Abbey and another in the churchyard of the Church of St John. The "original" Glastonbury Thorn was cut down and burned as a relic of superstition during the English Civil War, and one planted on Wearyall Hill in 1951 to replace it had its branches cut off in 2010. Further cuttings have been used to replace it again and of course there is still another off shoot of the original bush which is in Washington DC, USA.

Hereward the Wake

Hereward the Wake

I never ceased to be impressed by some of the early British characters and their battles for freedom. Hereward the Wake was a half Dane who was also part of the Saxon Royal family. He was involved in a battle, in the year 1070, which was probably one of the final attempts to keep England as the Normans advanced throughout the British Ilses and Ireland.

Had Abbot Thurston not committed an act of Treason against the English then arguably Ely may not have fallen to the French......but there would have been another day and another fight someplace else maybe....

Hereward the Wake

Exile of Hereward the Wake

Hereward was born most wild and rough,
wayward and made of much stronger stuff,
but exiled from England by Edward the King,
for he and Hereward argued all things.

Born of Earl Loefric and Godiva the wife,
by the age of fourteen Hereward was strife,
so Edward the King sent him away,
far off to Europe and there he would stay.

Death of King Harold

Now when Harold the King lay to his death,
Hereward's father felt much bereft,
not just for a King but the loss of his lands,
the Normans took all and left nought but strands.

So hearing his father was left with nought,
Hereward came to England with one mighty thought,
to smash all known Normans and leave them damned,
and take for his family the lands they'd been banned.

(Continued Overleaf)

Hereward Fights for England

Upon now reaching his old family's home,
he stood back and stared at what he'd been shown,
for there over the doorway; his brother's head,
nailed there by the Normans to show him as dead.

Flying into rage he drew forth his sword,
and in manic madness spun round and sought,
all known Normans in charge of this home,
and struck them down right to the bone.

Fourteen Norman French were cut down that day,
by this mad manic man so that he could now stay,
in his old home as was once before,
but now fourteen heads hung from the door.

So Hereward ran far; for to the Fens,
to gather support and meet with his friends,
protected by an Abbot; Thurston of old,
he sat and decided; we must be more bold!

The Battle of Peterborough

Reinforced with armies of Estrithson the Dane,
who came now to Ely to put Normans to shame,
Hereward fought for a Cathedral to see,
in old town Peterborough his people to free.

Having taken their Peterborough Church,
Hereward paid the Danes to disperse,
and the Danes headed back to their lands over sea,
with gold from Peterborough for all to see.

The Betrayal of Abbot Thurston

This enraged Abbot Thurston so sore,
so the Abbot betrayed to even the score,
why should Danish have gold from his church?
So he turned against Hereward who was left in the lurch.

Leading the Normans by a secret way,
to the Isle of Ely ; with Hereward in dismay,
Abbot Thurston led the Normans in,
and finally their army started to win.

Hereward the Recluse

Hereward now ran for the woods of the fens,
and for years he sat in renegade dens,
hidden from all by a renegade force,
friends of the rough lands all loyal of course.

Eventually one day King William found,
Hereward would deal; a solution to astound,
King William gave Hereward his lands,
but no more was England as all was now banned.

The Songs I Once Knew

The Songs I Once Knew

Throughout the teenage years of angst and getting to know one's self , and one's way in the world, there is a constant companion. The campanion is music and youth culture music makes for a very strong impression within the various tribes and styles of teenage culture. I ordered a copy of an old Emerson Lake and Palmer CD that I used to like recently. It was from the year 1972. I liked it when I was at primary school, I liked it when I was a teenager, and I still like it now.

The Songs I Once Knew

The songs I once knew faded away,
and the tunes we had; chose not to stay,
sometimes I think of what went wrong,
for not to lie; they never sang our song.
Memories of the road to your door,
fade to the depths of memories store,
remembrance of your warm embrace,
but you were so sure that you needed space.
So I'll sing you a song of the mists of dawn,
and the magic of twilight over a field of corn,
the winds that whisper high in the trees,
of all that is good and all a man sees.
That photo still sits of your wedding dress,
never forgotten since all of life's mess,
the distant horizon shows a far distant sun,
so when is it over and what have we won?

Esther

Esther

This is a poem about Esther. Esther was a friend of mine up until about my 18th birthday when shortly after she died. She was of an Irish family and was born with dwarfism. What God took away from her in height he made up for by making her more intelligent and sophisticated than the people around her. Esther was not poor or somebody to be pitied. Her family made provision so that she would be always cared for by making her the owner, as a child, to a large detached family property which was probably about 8 bedroomed. Also a second property which was a detached bungalow. She owned the lot as ownership was assigned to her name. Far from being sympathetic to her local people in her area used to call her a little rat to her face and insult her all of the while. The matter came to a head when she had a her neck twisted and was murdered just before coming of age. Where ever Esther went she rode on a small bicycle with stabilisers. The reason for the stabilisers was that she could get around speedily indoors and not just use the bicycle for outside purposes. So this is a poem to my memory of my friend Esther; and to my memory of the disgusting, appalling, local people that she had to put up with in the area that she was brought up in.

Esther

The streets had an echoing sound of small wheels,
till life was crushed under fates own heels,
such a large smile from a girl so small.
but it came from the heart and that was all.
No thoughts of greed or jealous strife,
just a small smile from one fated in life,
so when she fell with her life broken,
there was no more to say for it was all spoken.
The clank of her bike still echoes round halls,
a glimmer of past flickers and calls,
is life really so "just" to take one so pure,
or is life a war with no real cure?
The people around called her a rat,
and her heart was ripped from start to the last,
but I saw my friend and protected her true,
let the people rot they were nothing to you.
As night draws in to a darkened hall,
a noise of small wheels grows and calls,
for the justice of time to render a cure,
and the ghost of a child appears so pure.
This image it flickers sometimes or not,
to those who stole from her all that she'd got,
but I knew real Esther who sat in my car,
we knew who's right though she's now afar.
So let the dawn break as the people arise,
they called her a rat so now she'll despise,
your haunted street echoes for all time,
in the darkness she'll come for all of your crimes.

Across The Moors

Across The Moors

Flowering heather of the Moors. My favourite flowering plant and one that I take with me in plant posts where ever I live. Remember that old classic song by the Byrds Rock Band called Wild Mountain Thyme? It was based on a classic Scottish folk song and brings the power of the wilderness of nature well and truly home. Wandering across the heather covered moors is where I should be right now.

Across The Moors

Across the moors in the heather blooming,
wild birds scatter and abandon grooming,
taking to the skies higher in fright,
while the purple heather blows in spite.

The wind weaves circles whilst the sheep now bleat,
and I trample on with boot clump feet,
bracken and thistle then marshland crossed,
whilst the clouds cross by with the wind now tossed.

Whistle the wind and hum me a song,
a song to the bower where the sheep lie long,
and new born lambs now skip and prance,
dancing the rhythm of nature's trance.

The trance of life with the beat of a heart,
primordial beat born at the start,
a Kestrel glides from a vantage high,
whilst fleeing sparrows take to the sky.

The Skylark hovers warbling with might,
then ascends a hundred right out of sight,
brown mice bob and scatter most quickly,
clouds draw grey and move in thickly.

The change from sun to rain is coming,
so back to our car we start the running,
but oh the joy of scent as we go,
the perfume of heather that all of us know.

Do You Believe?

<u>Do You Believe?</u>

I wrote these four lines because I suddenly got the urge to.....I didn't want it to be any longer than four lines because it says what I want it to say and then ends.....It doesn't really need to say any more than it does say. The subject of the inner self, and what it is, is an interesting subject:-

Do You Believe?

Do you believe in a mystic light,

transcending our soul with inner sight,

do you believe all the soul can know,

an inner peace with a warmest glow.

Rhiged of the Celts (Celtic Cambric Kingdom of Cumbria)

Rhiged of the Celts (Celtic Cambric Kingdom of Cumbria)

Rhiged was the Celtic Country of northern Britain that went on to become what is approximately Cumbria in it's final smaller form. It's final King did not cease to rule until the year 945 ACE. Rhiged marks a number of small Celtic Kingdoms that carried on well after the Romans vacated the British Isles. The most recent being Cornwall which only ceased to be a separate country a few hundred years ago. This poem is About Rhiged and one of it's rulers King Urien . King Urien was a direct descendant of King Cole.

Rhiged of the Celts (Celtic Cambric Kingdom of Cumbria)

The Fell winds blew across the ridge top,
and the horses so wild gathered to stop,
a fire in the valley with warriors around,
awaiting the King of Brigantia as found.

In the distance Blencathra the Devil's own peak,
brothers of the valley in Cumbo do speak,
oh the Cambric tongue of the Rhiged tribes,
whilst the spirit of the water draws such
ancient vibes.

King Urien their King and descendant of Cole,
Cole Hen the Strong or Cole Hen the Old,
Urien the bringer of peace to Welsh tribes,
Dun Rhiged his fort where Celtic strength hides.

Uniting the Welsh from their squabbles and strife,
Urien pushed Saxons in fear for their life,
way back to the coast and over the sea,
but the victory was short for killed was he.

(Continued Overleaf)

Leader of Rhiged and the whole of Wales,
but after his victory his life finally fails,
for the jealous King Morcant struck him down,
wanting the Welsh for his own army's Crown.

The Welsh turned away and again all was lost,
The Saxon leaders took all with no cost,
Rhiged struggled for centuries to come,
till in 945 it was England that won.

King Dunmail of Rhiged the last Cambric King,
slaughtered in battle and lost everything,
but a cairn of stones now marks the site,
the end of old Rhiged and strong Celtic might.

Notes:-

Rhiged was the Celtic Country of northern Britain that went on to become
Cumbria in it's final smaller form. Rhiged was first united by King Cole Hen
who is best known within the nursery rhyme "old King Cole". The Cambric
language was close enough to the Brythonic Welsh language for Cumbria
people to be able to speak to Welsh tribes within their native tongue.

The descendant of King Cole, called King Urien, proved to be the most
powerful of the line of Cambric Monarchy. This was because from Cumbria
he managed to unite warring tribes in Wales into one united army which he
used to then successfully attack the migrant Saxon forces in what was to
become England later on in 925 ACE.

He was so successful in his attack on Anglo-Saxon forces that the Saxon army
retreated all of the way to the south coast and headed back over seas,

His victory was short lived because King Morcant, of Din Eiden, which later on became Edinburgh had become jealous. In a fit of jealous rage he arranged to meet King Urien and struck him down and ran him through dead. His reason was that he, King Morcant, felt that the Welsh armies should serve him in Scotland and not the Cambric Celts of Rhiged.

The Welsh armies once again started to fight each other over trivial matters without their King Urien to unite them. The Saxons returned and took over Rhiged for the Anglo-Saxon country with few problems without the strong King Urien there to defeat them with his united tribal army.

After the death of King Urien the Royal House of Rhiged continued for a few centuries in a weak state. Then in the year 945 ACE the final King of the Cambric Celts called King Dunmail was finally slaughtered and the Royal House of Rhiged came to an end. His defeat was by a united attack from both King Malcolm of Scotland on one side and King Edmund of England on the other side.

A Cairn of stones was ordered to be erected at the exact location that King Dunmail was slaughtered in battle. To this day the cairn of stones is still there and marks the end of the Celtic Kingdom called Rhiged in 945 ACE.

Eye in the Sky

Eye in the Sky

This my second Cinquain poem (pronounced Sin-Cain). Because I fancied a change of style for this poem. The Cinquain is a type of poem first invented by Adelaide Crapsey around a century ago in the USA. The Cinquain has set rules as to how it should be written:-

* Cinquain poems must be 5 lines long.

* A Cinquain poem has 2 syllables on the first line, 4 on the second, 6 on the third, 8 on the 4th, and 2 syllables on the 5th line.

* Cinquain poems do not need to rhyme but can if you want.

Eye in the Sky

Proud Sky
above us all
inner sight sure to call
sky and soul blend and flow till gone
as one

Caractacus of the Britons

Caractacus of the Britons

King Caractacus ; A legendary King known best in a song once sung by Rolf Harris but also a real person in history. The final battle of King Caractacus, against the Roman Empire, at Caer Caradoc, is known to have been at a site in Shropshire , England. Nobody has ever managed to identify which one of several fortified mound areas did the battle actually occur at though.

Caractacus of the Britons

Swords and spears and battle horse cries,
charging on with hair blown high,
body paint carefully pre prepared,
and drums that beat the rhythm shared.
Caractacus the Lord of might,
ran with the wind at its height,
horns that blew the triumph charge,
played the tune of rampant barge.
Though sweet the taste of battle seemed,
short did it last as the Romans schemed,
at Caer Caradoc he finally fell,
and his wife and children snatched to sell.
Of Rome their captive people knew,
so Caractacus he ran and flew,
for a distant Kingdom to the north,
Queen Cartimandua held with force.
Once arrived he felt so much dismay,
he was chained and they sent that very day,
for Rome to take him by arrest,
and charge him for his barbarous zest.
So to Rome did they take Caractacus,
and Claudius spoke without a fuss,
but Caractacus gave a speech so grand,
Claudius freed him with a wave of hand.
So free to wander in Rome's own glory,
Caractacus wrote this very story.

Notes

It never ceases to amaze me how every success of the Roman Empire in British early history, as written by the Roman historian Tacitus even, turns out to achieve the opposite a little later on in time.

The tale of King Caractacus (AKA Caradoc) is one such example. He won so many battles against the Roman Empire, in Britain, that his defeat, in armed warfare, became the main priority of the Roman Empire in the west territories.

Having finally defeated King Caractacus at the Battle of Caer Caradoc King Caractacus fled for protection to the Brigante Kingdom (now partly Yorkshire) to the North of England/Albion. Here Queen Cartimandua decides to hand the poor man over to the Empire of Rome instead of offering him protection. So off to Rome he is taken in chains.

Upon reaching Rome Caractacus gave a speech so eloquent, and sophisticated, that Emperor Claudius forgave him for every single thing that he did in battle and granted him complete freedom of the city of Rome to wander around as he pleased. Caractacus's children then went on to become anointed saints of the Roman Empire having helped to take Christianity to Britain. The whole family of Caractacus went back to being Royals of Britain, by 7 years later on, and in charge of the areas of their people that they were originally defeated in. Some of them married to Roman Senators and some holding ancient British Royal titles again.

This is the basis of the speech that King Caractacus, of the Ancient Britons, gave to Emperor Claudius to win his freedom:-

"If the degree of my nobility and fortune had been matched by moderation in success, I would have come to this country as a friend rather than a captive, nor would you have disdained to receive with a Treaty of Peace one sprung from brilliant ancestors and commanding a great many nations. But my present lot, disfiguring as it is for me, is magnificent for you. I had horses, men, arms, and wealth: what wonder if I was unwilling to lose them? If you wish to command everyone, does it really follow that everyone should accept your slavery? If I were now being handed over as one who had surrendered immediately, neither fortune nor your glory would have achieved brilliance. It is also true that in my case any reprisal will be followed by oblivion. On the other hand, if you preserve me safe and sound, I shall be an eternal example of your clemency"

Rainy Day Times – No's 3, 4 and 5

Rainy Day Times – No's 3, 4 and 5

Rain rain go away come back again on washing day....Bored bored bored!.....Rain rain rain! Bored bored bored! What should I do if it is too wet to go out? Write a poem about it of course!

<u>Rainy Day Times –</u>
<u>No's 3, 4 and 5</u>

The sound of splashing drives me out of my brain,
I can't stand the sound and it causes such pain,
let the clouds draw in grey and swallow the sky,
as my room draws in dark from the vexed clouds so high.
Rattling and tattling on the bin lid so loud,
filling the gutter and gushing to ground,
torrents with warrants invading my time,
swirling and twirling so watery fine.
Rat a tat tat all the way down the door,
winds growing louder to even the score,
blossom blown scattered all over the lawn,
drenched in a soaking with new rain drops born.
Drains gurgle loudly by roadside kerbs,
driving on harder on poor rain soaked birds,
just cancel that rattle of roof top slates,
I really can't stand this din that "me hates".

Cosmic Journey

Cosmic Journey

Memories of watching the night sky stars, and moon, are what inspired this poem. Memories of Spanish bars and the Cicadas scratching noisily outside in the darkened scrub. The stark darkness of the sky outside of the bar on a remote Spanish Island location with no street lighting outside. The stars glow even brighter without the street lighting....beautiful!

Cosmic Journey

Look to the stars for the sign of the Plough,
the North Star is there to show us how,
now follow me on to the Milky Way,
constellations beyond before the new day.
Sparkling in darkness of Andromeda's sight,
Cygnus found in the darkest night,
Aquila saw the plight of Lyra,
Hercules lifted the star disc so clearer.
Ursa Minor and Cassiopeia.
Awaiting the hour of Perseus near,
spinning, revolving, round and around
Vega and Deneb a sight to astound.
This dark cloth of gems revolves to my gaze,
Scorpius appears as Antares we praise,
ring out the bells for the star gaze dance,
sing to the sparkle of light show trance,
Sirius points to Canis Major,
Andromeda smiles like some long lost stranger,
and now in the middle of all sit I,
a mind spinning round with star light shine.

The Oins of Nark

The Oins of Nark

This is a poem about those small invisible people that we have all heard of. Yes, of course, the Oins of Nark! The Oins of Nark once hid in the park, I once met an Oin on a darkened stair, he was sitting most quiet and not to scare!........Errr... erm....... I'll get on with the poem then.

The Oins of Nark

When the Oins of Nark rise from the dell,
of this I've told you and told you well,
beware their stare whilst out in the dark,
and wait for their call to the free one of Sark.
Whilst out on the moors watch your time,
for the Nark of Sark it is no crime,
to rise above all with a chilling cry,
and gamble their gaudles high upon high.
Gangling slowly you'll reach the park,
but the Nark will gimble calling your heart,
to feel for the strangeness of faraway lands,
and leave you shaking with jabbert like hands.
Your gibberts now gangle far from the dell,
and though you worry no one can tell,
hiding from Oins but they whisper so clear,
we know where you are and we shall you fear!

Just a Photograph

Just a Photograph

For a while, back in time, I used to be interested in 35 mm photography. Then one day I realised I was only mediocre and really not especially any good at it. Then a few years went by and digital technology took over from 35 mm film. So I abandoned any idea of a photography as a hobby, sold my SLR 35 mm camera, and bought a digital snap shot camera the same as everyone else. I still love looking at good photography though. This poem is about reminiscing over an old photograph.

Just a Photograph

A picture of how we used to be. Just a flicker of time in print. Colours and shapes and shades; you looked so young and so did I. Aspiring and yearning and reaching out for thoughts in the sky; some hidden behind clouds. Thoughts of what we wanted, what we felt we should be, what we felt we were.Then time drifted and slid so quickly.

Where are the two spectres of that image now? Were they us? Were they us then? Are they still us now? Maybe a flame burns lightly deep inside for the both of us; or maybe that flame just burns quietly in spite of us.

Don't speak loudly lest the flame flickers and finally dies. Don't speak harshly lest the final warm ashes of our memory take to the breeze and scatter on the grass randomly under your breath. Don't speak at all; just sit and watch and wonder. Then quietly turn from me and go.

216

Time Tracked

Time Tracked

The passage of time. Images and flickers in the mind, of past and present, and dreamed images of the future. Memories and wishes. Desires and hates. Are you who you wanted to be? What do you intend to be in the future? How do other people see you now? That is what this poem is about.

Time Tracked

The old bell chimed though it's strike was slow,
and the old man limped against the flow,
then somehow time seemed to miss a beat,
with no rhyme or reason in the city street.
Somewhere through a shining light,
beckoning on to it's distant sight,
all that dazzles in a future scene,
far from the old town where I had been.
Memories fade though we try so keen,
to only remember the good times been,
and wipe away all the bad times gone,
as if some how this will make us strong.
Looking at clouds in a darkened night,
swirling around the church spires height,
and still somehow inside I see,
the distant past; it was the key.
So we wear our smiles like a grease mask face,
setting standards in social grace,
but when the waxy grease it cracks,
it scars so deep and the pain attacks.
I'll arise and go to a distant shore,
and leave old time to think some more,
somewhere between before and beyond,
and all the things I was so fond.
The old bell chimed though it's strike was slow,
and the old man limped against the flow,
then somehow time seemed to miss a beat,
with no rhyme or reason in the city street

Acknowledgement

For some time now I have been living in the county of Northamptonshire. I once read, somewhere or other, that Northamptonshire is county of squires and spires and rose of the shires. I have memories of the Northamptonshire Countryside going back to 1969 but it is recent times that I need to be grateful for. The rolling fields and countryside of Northamptonshire have granted me the inspiration to complete a number of books of poetry which have now been published. Where ever I find myself living in the future it is Northamptonshire, that I thank, for the successful publication of my books of poetry.

Made in the USA
Charleston, SC
01 August 2016